RELATIVE SANITY

POEMS

ELLEN LORD

Modern History Press
Ann Arbor, MI

Relative Sanity.
Copyright © 2023 by Ellen Lord. All Rights Reserved.

Cover art by Wendi Wright.
Interior illustrations by Joanna Walitalo.

ISBN 978-1-61599-767-1 paperback
ISBN 978-1-61599-768-8 hardcover
ISBN 978-1-61599-769-5 eBook

Modern History Press   www.ModernHistoryPress.com
5145 Pontiac Trail   info@ModernHistoryPress.com
Ann Arbor, MI 48105   Tollfree 888-761-6268

Distributed by Ingram (USA, CAN, UK, EU, UAE)

Contents

Muse 1

I 3
    Relative Sanity 4
    Raven's Child 5
    Music 6
    An Elegy 7
    East Branch Rainbow 8
    Going Home 9
    Yearn 10

II 11
    Another Covid Dream 12
    Who Will Wash Him Clean? 13
    He Survived a Gunshot Wound to the Head 14
    Dark 16
    Guillotine Dream 17
    Therapist's Dilemma 18
    Dead Husbands 19

III 21
    Lumberjack Tango 22
    Fickle Moon 23
    Angst 24

IV 25

- Two Riders 26
- Blues 27
- The Biker's Wife 28
- Ode to Blue 29
- Summer Heat 30
- Sky Dance 31
- Eros 32
- Forest Bathing (Shin Rin Roku) 33
- Fish Tale: An Elegy 34
- Post Harvest Lament 35
- Interlude 36
- Just A Moment 37
- Seasonal Angst 38
- New Widow 39
- Gypsy Valentine 40
- North Country Elegy 41
- Blursday 42
- Acknowledgements 43
- About the Author: 45

To Edd for—you know—this

Muse

—*after W.S. Merwin*

Searching for words
very early, I sense a kind of sighing
close by
like a rippled pond or stand of aspens in the dark.
I am reminded
of the mystery of every fleeting thought
I have forgotten
trusting a syllable will surface
from the depths of silence.

Relative Sanity

      --- for Jean Mary

In my dream mother waits for me. Her room exudes old-world charm, classic books, high ceilings, multicolored masks and Merino glass shimmers in afternoon light.

She sits curled in a leather chair, barefoot in a cotton dress, young with long auburn hair and bottomless eyes. In her distracted loveliness, she doesn't look like the woman I remember. She smiles as I approach and then softly fades away.

Later, I have visions of her escape from Newberry State Hospital. She was thirty-three years old with five children. An 'involuntary commitment' put her there after she tried to tame a nervous breakdown with gallons of blackberry wine. It was in the autumn of 1957. The weather was turning cold.

She never told me how she breached locked doors and caged windows but she hitchhiked two hundred miles in hospital garb and worn slippers. She would later recall, "The nicest folks gave me a ride and it was the best time I had in a long while. I felt reckless and wild."

The night she got home, I awakened to lights flashing in the driveway. Police had arrived. She locked herself in the bathroom and we could hear the shower running. She spoke calmly through the door. "I'll come out when I'm damn well ready."

They took her back to the asylum; she didn't return home that year. We would drive to see her on weekends, Lake Michigan iced and roiling along U.S. 2. She gave us moccasins and braided lanyards from art therapy. I don't remember saying goodbye but I recall the long, quiet rides home.

                    asylum seeker
            dancing barefoot and childless
                     in another life

Raven's Child

He arrived in July, the last of five
nearly aborted, then saved.
A withered miracle,
Mama's desperado child.

In the sultry, summer morning
she nursed him like her last hope.
A perfect doll for our jaded queen—
It was a troubled house.

I would walk the back fields,
wisps of meadow grass swaying
in afternoon sunlight, then ease
into a deep tangle of forest.

Here, I came upon the
carcass of a Guernsey cow.
She lay bloated in a swamp,
milky eyes frozen in time.

I wonder what she saw
as her weary legs buckled,
her shriveled udder sagging
into the murky fen.

I hoped scent of wildflowers
carried her bovine spirit up
like a solitary raven
destined to nest on the moon.

Music

> *"True singing is a different kind of breath.*
> *A breath about nothing. A blowing in the god.*
> *A wind."* — Rilke, The Sonnets to Orpheus, I, 3

My first music was mother's heartbeat,
a pulsing 1:2 rhythm; her laughter, a sigh,
or deep sob when she thought she was alone.

I love the timeless lyrics of lullabies—
rock a bye sweet darlin'. Yes,
I would rather be blind than lose the sensation of sound.

Music is the backstory to my changes,
memory's muse mapped in melody,
ethereal symphony to delicious guttural blues—and more;
the swoon with the seasons in treble or bass.

George Winston's piano will make me weep
and what of Bob Dylan, Dylan, Dylan.
we came 'of age' together and *may we stay forever young—*

Today, the rain played a laughing song on the tin roof
of my garden shed, a percussion of thunder, a flash of light.
Bring on the music of storms, the tempo of wind,
the luscious fermata of silence.

Let me dance. May the grand finale for me, for you, for us…
be a breath, a heartbeat, applause.

An Elegy

> *—after Ted Kooser*

In autumn, after summer's heat
has released the harvest,
golden silk of ripe corn ripples
in the evening air. A field mouse
pauses by a pile of stone to watch
a wizened farmer as he leans
against his mended fence.
His face is lined with the seasons
and his leathered hands are still.
But you must know, that raven
will continue to call, deer
in the pinewoods will be restless,
and coyote in deep tangle
of swamp will wait, long-legged
and patient as winter's chill.

East Branch Rainbow

Ontonagon River
iron-hued gush and surge
feeds a verdant forest.
Trout dives deftly
to silky depths—
surges up
glistening.

Going Home

— for Guss

I still have a vision of his eyes
in the glow of day down
as he turned towards the sound
of geese flapping, raucous on the lake.
Once, as a child,
my father spoke to me
of the migratory pattern of birds
the way their seeming chaos
became the flow of primitive belonging.
Lately, I lose myself
in cloudscapes, floating
endlessly toward a dream—
until the sky becomes a palette
for memories of going home.

Yearn

> *"If anyone understood loneliness,*
> *the moon would."*
> —Kaya

try to touch the sky
dark eyes search far-fleeting clouds
try to hold the rain
why does the mockingbird sing
desire lingers at dusk

wait like a perched bird
anchored in a high-sway wind
longing to depart
yet reluctant to let go
no mate to compass her home

why is it that she
yearns to marry the nightbird
unrequited muse
watchful orb of the wolf moon
waxes, then wanes in her eyes

II

Another Covid Dream

> —*after Federico Garcia Lorca*

A white dove goes flying
far away—

Dawn is red
in my dream
and dark thoughts sink
like stones
in a deep river.
I want to go back
to the day you were singing
as the tea steeped in the cup—
But now, I stand
on the shore of a virulent sea,
and there is sorrow on the wind.
How many golden hours does death have?
I will mourn them all.

A raven comes flying
into this day—

Who Will Wash Him Clean?

—for M.L.

At the end of the day, I sit
at my desk as Michael walks in.
He smells of coffee, cigarettes,
and a long day's toil.
I counseled him years ago
after he got out of prison.
Did a 20-year-bit for armed robbery,
said *the gun wasn't loaded*—
that kind of desperation.
He tells me the cancer is back, creeping
through him like Kudzu.
He feels it in the night, deep
inside his bones, as silence settles in.
He's done with chemo now,
wants one more summer—
hopes to live to the end of the year.
In the meantime, he still has to work a bit,
take care of Ma and tend to that old dog.
I ask him *is there something special*
you want, you know, before you go?
He says *I can't think of anything,*
just need spring to come, tired
of the chill and piles of dirty snow.
I want to feel the sun on my face,
see summer roll in lazy and hot,
a soft breeze on my skin—
I want to look up one last time,
into a cleansing rain.

He Survived a Gunshot Wound to the Head

—for Dave

I stepped into his madness as he walked into the room.
His brows were pierced with stainless spikes.
I thought he smelled of fire.
He spoke of lightning and ravens' wings.

His brows were pierced with stainless spikes.
His eyes shot sparks that he caught in his hand.
He spoke of lightning and ravens' wings.
I was told he had seizures in jail.

His eyes shot sparks that he caught in his hand.
He said he was a disciple of Thor.
I was told he had seizures in jail.
I sat by the window as he stood by the door.

He said he was a disciple of Thor.
He would run in the night by a lake in the woods.
I sat by the window as he stood near the door.
He cried when he spoke of being locked in a cage.

He would run in the night by a lake in the woods.
His tattoos were a map of his world.
He cried when he spoke of being locked in a cage.
I heard the lost child in his voice.

His tattoos were a map of his world.
He believed he had been a warrior king.
I heard the lost child in his voice.
He died on a boarding house floor.

He believed he had been a warrior king.
I stepped into his madness as he walked into the room.
He died on a boarding house floor.
I thought he smelled of fire.

Dark

— *after Jericho Brown*

His silhouette loomed under a cold moon.
He was a traveler, restless with desire.

He was a traveler reckless with desire.
His obsessive nature mirrored my own.

My moods mirrored his own obsessive nature.
The heat of his yearning consumed me.

The heat of my yearning consumed him.
There was always a desire for fire.

There was a manic desire, a smoldering fire.
He carried danger inside, a brooding bloom.

Guillotine Dream

What I took to be a piece of chocolate
turned out to be a severed sow's ear,
petrified and shriveled in a crystal dish.
What I took to be a blazing sunrise,
turned out to be the flame-glow of a wildfire
set by vandals in my cherished forest.
And what I took to be your tears of remorse,
turned out to be an outpouring of rage
as you turned and stormed away.
It was my love-sick brain, intoxicated
with the illusion of your charismatic guile
that turned out to be the devastating finale
of a psychotic interlude.
And, so it was—
a general misunderstanding of the world,
denial of insidious malice and misperception
of dark motives, more tragic than comic.
that precipitated my decision to sever
the heads of your cherished tulips.

Therapist's Dilemma

I had a reputation for being
the one to see when life got too full
of flummox and heartache.
A woman called me on Sunday,
tear-talking, said her lover had left,
couldn't turn off the bad thoughts.
She spoke of years of betrayal.
We made an appointment for the next day.
She arrived late and, surprisingly,
did not seem at all undone. She floated
onto the couch and crossed her legs.
Who wears high-heel shoes these days?
"He leaves, comes back, leaves."
"Does he tell you why?"
"He's evasive. I always take him back
 but I want to do something different this time."
"What do you think you should do?"
"Well, I thought I'd ask you. He's your husband."

Dead Husbands

At night they step out from the shadows.
to enter the house of her dreams,
ruminate on broken promises,
rant-chant a litany of sins.

They wave divorce decrees,
sepia photographs of times
taken before the mean season
when hearts throbbed with desire.

They discuss death certificates,
argue about final diagnosis,
correct eulogies and re-file regrets.
They always stay too long.

Righteous rants urge her
to pay attention, to fasten
her top buttons, to throw away
those high-heeled shoes.

And all the while, she yearns
to flow away in scarlet silk,
a sultry slide, a grand finale—
beyond the exit door.

III

Lumberjack Tango

Dance with me
make me sway—
kiss me on the lips.

How tall are you?

Bend me into your dreams
let's shimmy, shimmy along
well beyond midnight.

Let me wear your hat.

Fickle Moon

Once upon a time,
I lie with my true love du jour
awed, then underwhelmed
as dawn hid my wishing star.
I picked him out at midnight
from a cast of guitar guys.
Oh, how he swayed—
Levi jeans, scarred boots, black hat.
My name, sweet like raw
honey from his lips.
Sometimes, the moon is a liar,
she tells me I'm queen of the night.
But I wax lonesome as she wanes—
crooning *shine on baby, shine on.*

Angst

Call me when you get there,
pleads the man by the iron gate.
He could make me happy,
He just needs to try.

Sometimes I pretend I am a stranger
in a jazz joint,
watching this man drink.

Dirty martini,
black flies on the bar.
I do not know where I am going
or if it really matters—

How many times a day should I call?

IV

Two Riders

> *"There must be some way out of here*
> *said the joker to the thief"*.
> — *Bob Dylan*

We left Ann Arbor at dawn
on a long rising road in Michigan—
shotgun cased and slung.
We hitched US 23, going north
to hunt at his camp in Curran.
He yearned for something wild
I just wanted to steal away.
It was October, fall colors vibrant
in the hills. So eager for adventure,
we believed this could be our life—
His eyes flashed mischief
as wistful drivers waved goodbye.
Luck and rides came easy—
for I was young and he was beautiful.
What I remember most, is how sunlight
shimmered above the highway,
like we were traveling to a distant sea,
an unexplored horizon, so far away
from where we were destined to be.
It was a mid-semester college interlude—
two small town desperados,
trying to traverse a big town world
on a quest to be the right size.

Blues

—after Leonard Cohen

You provide the music
if you want to live here.
Do you like this poem?
I wrote it in a heartache
I can no longer recall.
Do you remember when we met?
I didn't know then
that you could dance—
it would have made all the difference.

The Biker's Wife

—after Dorianne Laux

She loved him most
when he returned from a long ride—
face wind-burned, hair wild,
leather jacket dusty, redolent
of backroads and cedar.
She would meet him by the gate
as he swung his leg from the bike.
An outlaw smile would find his eyes.
On the fieldstone porch
she would pull off his boots,
open his shirt, take the whole ride inside her—
the bottomless sky, the hard road,
vibrations of his rumbling engine surging
into twilight to carry him home.

Ode to Blue

Northern Lights. Beach glass. Ice Cave. Moon
Indigo. Spruce. Navy. Lagoon.

Grass. Political State. Cheese.
Friend of Red and White on a Michigan breeze.

Bird of Happiness. Crayfish. Dragonfly. Bog.
Robin's egg. Larkspur. Diamond. Fog.

A color to be tangled up in.

Lake of The Clouds on a sun-spangled day.
Flecks on trout. Ontonagon River after it rains.
Twilight. Heaven. Hoarfrost. Mist.

Valentine.

Ribbon of rainbow. High heeled shoes.
Wild girl's hair. Lavender. Velvet.   Her poem.

Lupine. Delphinium. Melancholy. Smoke.
Balloon. Feather. Cotton Candy. Punch.

Jeans. Tattoo. Merry-Go-Round Pony. Balls.
First boyfriend's bad-ass truck. His song.

Eyes of a certain outlaw.

Sky.

Summer Heat

— *after Jane Kenyon*

the cricket's
hypnotic mantra
settles into me

the night is humid and dark
humid and dark

then why
does my body vibrate
with thoughts of you

so eager
for this pending storm
this pending storm

Sky Dance

Dance with me please,
as if you were the dawn sky—
soft filigreed clouds
tangled in your hair.
Sing
and I will rumble toward you
as if I were a god of thunder—
fire of midnight lighting
sequined in my eyes.

Eros

these gnarled fingers
long to touch those fleeting clouds
elusive lover
remember how you gave me
violet lilacs in spring

Forest Bathing (Shin Rin Roku)

Soft fascination
interplay of leaves and light.
Let your mind wander
into the aspen's branches.
Splendor of dappled beauty.

To flow unfurled
raptor rides the solar wind.
Follow, just follow.
Bird song echoes in the mist.
Spring dreams radiate with dawn.

Unfettered hours
pulsate in primitive song.
Breathe into the sky's
kaleidoscope of color
humbled by the mystery.

Fish Tale: An Elegy

How my body arched—
his lure finding
its way in silky shadow
to pierce my lip
his filament taut and urgent
—and I rose
beyond the surging cascade
of a thunderous waterfall—
a quiver
of salmon colored dazzle
glorious in the mist.

Post Harvest Lament

Same stormy mood, different year.
Up and down past midnight, the usual suspects—
messy things; chores left undone;
cravings for sweets, alcohol and outlaws.
A deluge of bitter rain leaves the sky fogged,
a vague gray; it's hard to take a deep breath.
I go to the tired garden. Opium pods nod—
ready to harvest; I want to fall on my knees,
suck them dry, get high— and so, it goes.
Finally, we speak after an interlude of ire
and my mind clears to vagrant blue. I smile as two
juvenile raccoons eat fallen apples, think of old
orchards and the camaraderie of trees,
how they sway, flow together—
unencumbered now, without their leaves.
Harvest is done for another cycle.
I think about the serendipity of opportunity—
pause to give thanks for this quiet hour.
We reap—

Interlude

We awaken
to the November moon, still high
over long-shadowed forest—
a primal silence.
Stormed in the night,
traces of snow remain.
I am restless
after waves of watery dreams,
searching for you again—
an old desperation.
You always say...
I'm right here. I am right here.
We walk.
Aspens stand naked, unencumbered.
I find two feathers, a stone—
you look for deer sign.
I cherish the interlude between storms.
It's easier to breathe. Breathe.
You take my hand.
The sky says another squall is pending
but now, there is just enough breeze
to feel gently kissed by nature.
I love us most when we walk—
a resilient camaraderie, a prayer.

Just A Moment

Heavy hoarfrost this morning,
magic of the ordinary aglow at dawn.
All these moments that make up our lives
how we battle to hold back the darkness,
how it feels to be alone.
You step into a copse of aspens, silent—
your shadow strides beside you.
Song birds heard but not seen,
air suffused with memory,
how your wilderness of uncertainty
aches into bloom.

Seasonal Angst

I get so scattered,
could not recall the word 'amethyst'
and it's my favorite semi-precious stone.
It took hours, then just dropped in
like a belated guest. I worry
about mental decline, like that helps.
I float about this house, find comfort
in mindless chores, then pause
to gaze out into winter's forest.
I see tracks in snow: deer, rabbit, opossum—
fellow travelers doing their quiet work.
I hear crows, wonder why they never sound peaceful
but soften to see an eagle
spiral in full soar.
Mercy comes gently today, nature's reprieve
from chatter in my mind. I linger
by the window to watch. Wait.
It seems like I can never get enough sky.

New Widow

The tree guy is here to prune two plums,
perhaps a few pines, if he has time.
He is never in a hurry.
It was the old apple's turn last winter, her rebirth
in spring was such a delight. He's careful
with trees, takes time to ponder their bend and sway,
a kind of reverence. His hands urge
tender fractals to pulsate and reach for the sky.
He is a purveyor of light.
He tells me, year after year, you always look the same.
I accept this kindness and it makes my day.
I bake an apple pie, warm a pot of soup,
settle gently into the afternoon. I wish
the woodsman would choose to linger
but his work this year is done.
As I rise to thank him, he smiles and offers
plum branches for my fire.
I give him the pie.

Gypsy Valentine

---for Edd

He rises early to start coffee,
folds his cover back over the night.
I linger and listen as sounds of dawn
pulse from blue shadows.
I think about this good man
with his ragged heart and his
poet's hands, how he traveled
such a long way just to wish me
good morning.
As we sip the hot, dark brew
from old porcelain cups,
he asks me what I would like
to do today, and I answer—
This.

North Country Elegy

—after Jim Harrison

I love these raw winter nights,
a thousand critters you can't see
hibernate under a shroud of snow.
My memory takes me back to another life,
how we would skate a northern lake,
warmed by desire.
I was oblivious then to the mercy
solitude could bestow.
My body has been betraying me
for a long time now—
I'm not quite sure anymore
how I learned to be alone.

Blursday

        another blursday
   so much comes to me, then leaves
      dark sky, silence—love

Acknowledgements

The author is grateful to the following publications in which poems first appeared, sometimes in slightly different versions:

Bear River Anthology: "New Widow" and North Country Elegy"

Dunes Review: "Muse," "Blues", "Summer Heat" and "North Country Elegy"

Haiku Society of America: "Blursday" previously published as "Haiku #24"

Open Palm Print: "Raven's Child," and "He Survived a Gunshot Wound to the Head"

Peninsula Poets (PSM): "Muse", "Music", "An Elegy", "Dead Husbands", "The Biker's Wife", "New Widow" and "Gypsy Valentine"

R.K.V.R.Y. Online Quarterly: "Relative Sanity"

Traverse Area District Library/PNO: "Going Home", "Who Will Wash HimClean" and "Eros"

Modern History Press / *U.P.Reader*: "Two Riders", "Another Covid Dream", "GuillotineDream" and "Interlude"

Walloon Writer's Review: "Seasonal Angst", "Yearn", Lumberjack Tango", Forest Bathing" and "Fish Tale: An Elegy"

Deepest Gratitude to the Following

To Edd Tury, my beloved partner and first reader.

To the Fresh Water Poets: Susan Griffiths, Michael Hughes and Katherine Roth, for their inspiration, support and passion for poetry.

To the Charlevoices Writer's Group. You keep me humble.

To Kenn Grimes for his expertise in critiquing my work.

To my clients who have trusted me with their stories and their secrets.

To Jennifer Huder for her wise edits and enthusiastic guidance.

To Wendi Wright for the experimental digital art I used for the cover.

To Joanna Walitalo for the beautiful renderings of feathers used herein.

And finally, to Victor Volkman at Modern History Press for his patience and expertise.

About the Author

Ellen Lord began writing as a kid, first stirred to poetry by Edgar Allen Poe's raven and various morbid nursery rhymes. She is inspired by forays in nature, along with feasts and foibles of the human condition. She was raised in the wilds of the Upper Peninsula and often returns to her ancestral home. She is a behavioral health therapist, specializing in addiction and trauma. She resides in Charlevoix County and Trout Creek, Michigan. This is her first collection.

Printed in the USA
CPSIA information can be obtained
at www.ICGtesting.com
JSHW021925190823
46760JS00002B/161